SATURDAY NIGHT

LIVE

Shaping TV Comedy and American Culture

ARIE KAPLAN

TWENTY-FIRST CENTURY BOOKS / MINNEAPOLIS

Twenty-First Century Books
A division of Lerner Publishing Group, Inc.
241 First Avenue North
Minneapolis, MN 55401 USA

For reading levels and more information, look up this title at www.lernerbooks.com.

Main text font set in Gamma ITC Std Medium 11/15
Typeface provided by International Typeface Corp.

Library of Congress Cataloging-in-Publication Data

Kaplan, Arie.
    Saturday Night Live : shaping TV comedy and American culture / by Arie Kaplan.
        pages   cm.
    Includes bibliographical references and index.
    ISBN 978-1-4677-1086-2 (lib. bdg. : alk. paper)
    ISBN 978-1-4677-4795-0 (eBook)
    1. Saturday night live (Television program) I. Title.
   PN1992.77.S273K37 2015
   791.45'72—dc23   2013039469

Manufactured in the United States of America
1 - PC - 7/15/13

CONTENTS

INTRODUCTION
EDGY AND UNPREDICTABLE 5

CHAPTER 1
BRING YOUR CHARACTERS! 9

CHAPTER 2
DIVERSITY . . . "YEAH, THAT'S THE TICKET!" 21

CHAPTER 3
LIVE FROM NEW YORK, IT'S . . . POLITICS? 33

CHAPTER 4
I'M KRISTEN WIIG, AND YOU'RE NOT! 43

MORE ABOUT SATURDAY NIGHT LIVE 56
CATCHPHRASE QUIZ 56
FROM SECOND CITY TO *SNL* 57
SATURDAY WRITE LIVE 58
SOURCE NOTES 59
SELECTED BIBLIOGRAPHY 60
FURTHER INFORMATION 61
INDEX 62

The Not Ready for Prime Time Players were the launch cast of *Saturday Night Live*. Clockwise from bottom center are Bill Murray, John Belushi, Gilda Radner, Garrett Morris, Dan Aykroyd, and Laraine Newman. Jane Curtin is in the center of the group.

INTRODUCTION
EDGY AND
UNPREDICTABLE

"LIVE FROM NEW YORK, IT'S SATURDAY NIGHT!" Millions of Americans recognize these words as the line that ends the cold open (the opening sketch) in every episode of *Saturday Night Live (SNL)*, the popular NBC weekly television sketch comedy series. Like many Americans, you—and your parents—are probably familiar with Stefon, Drunk Uncle, the Target Lady, and the show's many other recurring characters. You probably also repeat some of the show's catchphrases, such as "More cowbell," "New York's hottest club is . . . ," "It's always something," and "Schwing!"

SNL isn't just a sketch comedy show. It's a TV series that has made obscure comedians famous, turned famous comedians into superfamous rock stars, and shifted the very idea of a sketch comedy show into something fresh, different—and even slightly dangerous. When you think of *SNL* comedians such as Tina Fey, Chris Rock, Eddie Murphy, Will Ferrell, John Belushi, Gilda Radner, Amy Poehler, Bill Hader, and Adam Sandler, you think of edgy and unpredictable humor. But comedic actors

In the Beginning: Creating Saturday Night Live

In 1975 NBC had a weak Saturday night lineup with poor ratings. The TV station needed to come up with an exciting show that would be more appealing to young people than going out with their friends. So the network tapped young television writer-producer Lorne Michaels to develop a hip, new comedy show for young viewers. Michaels created a show that took talent from comedy clubs (such as Catch a Rising Star in New York City), improvisational sketch comedy troupes (such as Second City in Chicago and the Groundlings in Los Angeles), and edgy, rebellious humor magazines aimed at young adults (such as *National Lampoon*). He fused all three styles of comedy to form a new type of sketch comedy show. By the beginning of its second season, *SNL* was a true phenomenon — the first hit show any TV network ever had at eleven thirty eastern time on a Saturday night.

Lorne Michaels, *far left*, was the brain child behind *Saturday Night Live*. He was the show's first producer and one of its writers. Here he is pictured in a 1992 group shot with *(from left to right)* Mike Myers as Wayne Campbell, rock megastar Bruce Springsteen, actor Tom Hanks, and Dana Carvey as Garth Algar.

Before *SNL* first aired in 1975, famous comedians who hosted sketch or variety shows on TV included old-school comedic actors such as Carol Burnett, Bob Hope, and Milton Berle. They were very funny but in a friendly, slightly cheesy, and . . . well . . . safe way. They said and

Carol Burnett was a standout comedian in an era in which the big comedic stars were men. In her popular television variety comedy show, *The Carol Burnett Show* (1967–1978), she often poked fun at classic books and movies. Here, in a 1967 episode, she hams it up in a spoof of the animated children's film *The Jungle Book*.

did the sort of things your great-grandparents would find funny, and they would never say anything controversial or risqué. They rarely dealt with issues such as racism, sexuality, politics, or drug abuse.

Saturday Night Live changed the way we think about comedians and comedy. The type of comedy that's written for and performed on *SNL* lets the audience know that it's okay to laugh at political scandals and celebrities who say offensive things in public and pop stars who are obsessed with themselves and TV commercials that take themselves way too seriously. *SNL* paved the way for other provocative and intelligent comedy shows such as *The Simpsons, The Daily Show,* and *Louie.* And *SNL* is still going strong. The 2014–2015 season marked the show's fortieth year on the air. But those are just the broad strokes. All good comedy, they say, is in the details.

In an ordinary living room set, Jane Curtin *(left)* as Prymaat Conehead, Laraine Newman as daughter Connie Conehead *(center)*, and Dan Aykroyd *(right)* as Beldar Conehead got laughs as alien characters in suburban America. While not cued in to many everyday customs, they loved cheap American beer and junk food.

CHAPTER 1
BRING YOUR
CHARACTERS!

SATURDAY NIGHT LIVE PERFORMERS usually come to the show from the worlds of stand-up comedy, live scripted sketch comedy, or improvisational comedy. In 1986, when stand-up comedian Victoria Jackson was about to audition for *Saturday Night Live,* the show's producers encouraged her to "bring all your characters." As part of the audition, she—and other performers since then—perform bizarre characters or celebrity impressions that they've developed during their years as comedic performers. If executive producer Lorne Michaels and the other *SNL* producers like the characters, they have a good chance of becoming part of the show. One of the things that makes *SNL* unique is that it has a rotating cast. Every so often, certain cast members leave the show to pursue other opportunities, and new cast members create new characters. During certain periods of the show's history, almost all the veteran cast members and writers left and were replaced with new ones. The show's producers know that without this fresh infusion of new characters, the show's established characters become stale and played out.

Different Ways of Getting Laughs

What is the difference between stand-up comedy, scripted sketch comedy, and improvisational comedy? In stand-up comedy, one comedian tells jokes directly to the audience, often (but not always) in the form of a comedic monologue. Scripted sketch comedy consists of short, funny sketches that are scripted beforehand and performed by two or more people. Improvisational comedy (also called improv) features sketches performed by two or more people. But in improv, the sketches are not scripted beforehand. The actors may have developed certain characters, situations, and concepts during rehearsals or in previous performances. However, improv performers thrive on spontaneity. They often ask audience members to suggest an occupation or a setting for their characters, to help the scene along.

"WE ARE FROM FRANCE": THE 1970s

Iconic characters from the show's early years include a samurai (played by John Belushi), the Coneheads (played by Dan Aykroyd, Jane Curtin, and Laraine Newman), and Roseanne Roseannadanna (played by Gilda Radner). John Belushi's samurai character was originally inspired by Toshiro Mifune, a famous Japanese actor of the 1950s and the 1960s. Mifune had starred as a Japanese samurai warrior in the legendary samurai film *Yojimbo* (1961), directed by Japanese filmmaker Akira Kurosawa. Belushi mimicked the look and mannerisms of the gruff, ornery warrior in the samurai sketches. However, Belushi didn't actually speak Japanese in the sketches. Instead, he shouted out meaningless gibberish as he pulled

In September 1978, John Belushi's samurai character goes disco in a skit spoofing the megahit movie *Saturday Night Fever* (1977).

out his sword in settings such as delicatessens, dry cleaners, divorce court, and other places in which a real samurai would never have found himself.

Then there were the Coneheads, a family of aliens from the planet Remulak, hiding in plain sight in suburban America. With absurdly pointed heads, a stiff walk, and high-pitched, stilted speech, Beldar (Aykroyd) and his wife Prymaat (Curtin) go through daily life without actually being recognized as outsiders. In the rare situations where "Earthlings" do ask about their origins, they claim, ridiculously, that they are from France. The Coneheads' daughter Connie (Newman), on the other hand, is totally assimilated into Earthling—and American—culture. She mostly talks like a typical American teen and sees her parents as total weirdos. With her classically conventional American first name, Connie Conehead was a satire of first-generation Americans, some of whom are embarrassed by the quaint, unhip customs and values of their immigrant parents. The sketch also mocked mainstream America and its ignorance of—even blindness to—global cultures.

An equally absurd character appeared frequently on *SNL*'s "Weekend Update" news section. Roseanne Roseannadanna, one of Gilda Radner's best-loved creations, was inspired by a real person—New York anchorwoman Rose Ann Scamardella. In her piece, Radner's character, like Scamardella, was supposed to talk about consumer

Gilda Radner's Roseanne Roseannadanna was a thorn in the side of any "Weekend Update" host. The joke was that Roseanne could be counted on to rant about anything—except the consumer affairs issue she was supposed to be addressing.

affairs issues. She started each sketch by reading a letter from a concerned citizen. But instead of responding to the complaint, she would launch into a completely unrelated discussion of belly button lint, warts, the inside of her own mouth, and other personal hygiene pet peeves. Radner herself came up with Roseanne Rosenannadanna's funny name by applying "The Name Game" song ("James James BoBames, Banana Fanna FoFames . . .") to the name Roseanne.

"YEAH, THAT'S THE TICKET!" THE 1980s

In the summer of 1980, Lorne Michaels resigned his post on the show after a creative disagreement with the network. All the cast members and most of the writers, many of whom had been with the show since the beginning, also jumped ship, deciding that it was time to pursue other projects. A new cast and writing staff were assembled, and a new lineup of characters appeared.

Eddie Murphy was a major breakout performer from this era. Many of his characters made fun of established pop culture clichés. For example, his recurring "Mr. Robinson's Neighborhood" sketch was a parody of *Mister Rogers' Neighborhood*, a public television children's show starring Fred Rogers. But Murphy's neighborhood was not safe and squeaky clean. Instead, he set his sketches in a ghetto, where he dealt with issues such as violence and poverty.

> [Eddie Murphy's] "Mr. Robinson's Neighborhood" . . . dealt with issues such as violence and poverty.

Even Eddie Murphy's impersonation of the animated character Gumby was a twist on an old showbiz cliché. The always chipper, youthful Gumby starred in his own stop-motion clay animation children's TV series during the 1950s and the 1960s. Created by animator Art Clokey, Gumby was an iconic character for a generation of kids, who loved his colorful toyland companions. However, Murphy parodied Gumby by playing him as a cigar-smoking, crotchety old-timer who was bitter, washed up, and resentful.

Lorne Michaels returned to *SNL* as executive producer in 1985 after settling his differences with the network. He cast a wide range of exciting new performers. One of these was Jon Lovitz, famous for playing sleazy, obnoxious characters such as Tommy Flanagan, the Pathological Liar. The tagline to any of Flanagan's famous lies was "Yeah, that's the ticket!" reassuring himself that his latest lie was plausible enough to be accepted as truth.

Dana Carvey excelled at impressions of real-life politicians and celebrities, such as President George H. W. Bush and movie star John Travolta. He also created new characters, such as the Grumpy Old Man, specifically for *SNL*. Carvey's characters were never gimmicky, one-note, or predictable. He was a catchphrase machine for the show. When people gathered at work or school the Monday morning after a Carvey sketch on *SNL,* they were likely to quote one of his characters. Among the most popular were these two:

- ### "Could it be . . . Satan?"
  Carvey played the title character in the "Church Lady" sketches about the prudish, judgmental host of a fictional talk show called *"Church Chat."* Whenever the Church Lady would discuss a sexually charged issue in politics, pop culture, or current events, she would ask who was causing such a shameful display of lust and temptation. Answering her own question, she would shout, "Could it be . . . Satan?"

Dana Carvey as the Church Lady delivered hilariously uptight diatribes on sexually charged issues. The character was one of many that have relied on cross-dressing as part of the humor.

- **"We want to pump . . . you up!"**

  Hans (Dana Carvey) and Franz (Kevin Nealon) were Austrian bodybuilders in the "Pumping Up with Hans & Franz" sketches. The catchphrase was part of their parody of popular Hollywood actor Arnold Schwarzenegger, known for his big muscles and Austrian accent.

Phil Hartman, often referred to as the glue that held the show together, was an *SNL* mainstay from 1986 until 1994. He created such amazing characters as Unfrozen Caveman Lawyer, a caveman who was frozen in ice one hundred thousand years ago. Recently thawed out, he attends law school and becomes a successful, articulate attorney. In sketches set in court, the Unfrozen Caveman Lawyer shrewdly manipulates the jury into believing he is frightened and confused by the modern world, as a way to gain sympathy and win his case. Hartman also played Frankenstein's Monster in the "Tonto, Tarzan, and Frankenstein's Monster" sketches and gave pitch-perfect impressions of singer Frank Sinatra and US president Bill Clinton. In fact, *SNL* fans are divided as to who did the better Clinton impression: Phil Hartman or Darrell Hammond, who joined the show in the mid-1990s.

FRAT BOYS AND CHEERLEADERS: THE 1990s

By the early 1990s, cast members such as Carvey, Dennis Miller, Jon Lovitz, and Nora Dunn had all left the show. Younger cast graduated to more central roles in the show's sketches. They brought with them a youthful, anarchic spirit. Carvey remarked, "My younger friends who were right behind me—David Spade, Chris Farley, and Adam Sandler— were bursting with energy. They'd been on the junior varsity two or three years and it just seemed like a natural time for them to take over the show."

Sandler, Farley, and Spade wrote and starred in sketches, many of which mocked authority. These were sketches created by (and *for*) a younger generation. Some viewers described it as "frat boy" humor, filled with crude language, easy laughs, and jokes about bodily functions. Beginning with the 1995–1996 season, yet another stable of new performers emerged to replace Farley, Myers, Sandler, and Spade. The new troupe was led by Will Ferrell, Darrell Hammond, Cheri Oteri, and Molly Shannon. Some of the characters that emerged during this period exhibited a touch of sadness. How could you not feel sympathy for the Spartan cheerleaders? Played by Will Ferrell and Cheri Oteri, the two characters fail the audition for their school's beloved East Lake High School Spartan cheerleading squad. Yet they feel such loyalty to the squad—and such a need to belong—that they show up at games uninvited, performing overly enthusiastic routines with awkward moves and chants. Eventually the duo shows up at chess tournaments, swim meets, and other events at which cheerleaders do not usually perform.

Will Ferrell as Craig Buchanan and Cheri Oteri as Arianna had a habit of showing up to cheer just about any event. In this skit from 1996, the pair gives their all at a Ping-Pong tournament.

Similarly, Molly Shannon—an important female *SNL* performer of the era—played Mary Katherine Gallagher, a moody, unpopular adolescent Catholic schoolgirl with very curious habits. For example, she acts out scenes from maudlin TV movies to express her deepest emotions. She flashes her underpants in seeming innocence and, when nervous, sticks her fingers into her armpits for a sniff. Mary Katherine Gallagher and the Spartan cheerleaders symbolized the awkward, tortured teenage years that most viewers could relate to, and they were an instant hit.

Live and Unpredictable

Saturday Night Live is also known for its musical guests. And because it is a live show, musical guests sometimes take off in unpredictable directions. The most famous instance occurred on October 3, 1992, when Irish pop singer Sinéad O'Connor performed a cover of Bob Marley's song "War." At the end of the song, she ripped up a photo of Pope John Paul II, then the head of the Roman Catholic Church. The gesture was intended to protest the child abuse epidemic in the Catholic Church. The reaction in the audience was stunned silence. Critical reaction was divided. While some saw O'Connor's stunt as a brave attempt to bring a serious issue to light, fellow pop star Madonna publicly denounced her. NBC received more than nine hundred phone calls during the next two days, most of them criticizing the Irish singer. O'Connor's appearance has yet to be topped as the most controversial musical moment in the show's history.

TARGET LADY AND MILEY: THE 2000s

Throughout the early years of the twenty-first century, many *SNL* sketches either made fun of the silliest aspects of American society or were hilarious because they were random and nonsensical. Premiering in the year 2000, the "Gemini's Twin" sketches kicked off the decade. A parody of the pop/R&B girl group Destiny's Child, Gemini's Twin includes Jonette (played by Ana Gasteyer), Britanica (Maya Rudolph), and a third member of the group (played by that week's celebrity host). The revolving third member of the group—which included Cameron

Diaz and Jennifer Lopez, among others—was a biting commentary on the frequent lineup changes that famously plagued Destiny's Child over the years. Jonette and Britanica also amused audiences by making up or by misusing words. "It's time to get musicational!" and "Our music comes from a very emotionary place" are classic examples of their style.

Most Americans know someone who loves shopping at discount retail stores just a little too much. Kristen Wiig's Target Lady character was a spoof of such people. Her Target Lady was a dowdy, shrill, none-too-bright cashier at a Target store. She was a bit too excited to be working at Target, and each time she rang up a customer, she became obsessed with one of the items the person was buying. She then abandoned her post to find that exact item for herself, leaving the customer behind.

Kristen Wiig as the Target Lady takes on a cross-dressing Justin Timberlake as a character named Peg in a 2009 sketch. Some of the humor of *SNL* characters derives from their obsessional, over-the-top approach to life.

In a continuation of *SNL*'s long tradition of spoofing pop stars and celebrities, Vanessa Bayer mocks pop singer–actress Miley Cyrus in "The Miley Cyrus Show" sketches, the first of which debuted in 2010. In the sketches, Bayer as Miley Cyrus is an overly enthusiastic and naive pop star who invites guests onto her show. She asks them a lightning-fast barrage of interview questions in one insanely long run-on sentence. The "Miley Cyrus Show" sketches are popular for the way in which they portray celebrities as out of touch with reality.

GOING DIGITAL

Saturday Night Live has embraced the digital age through its *SNL* Digital Shorts, which began in 2005. These funny (and often musical) video shorts—which include "Lazy Sunday," "Do The Creep," and "Laser Cats"—feature comedy in short bursts that can be shared easily through video-sharing sites such as YouTube and Vimeo. The *SNL* Digital Shorts have involved many *SNL* writers and performers, such

In a January 2011 episode, pop star Nicki Minaj was *SNL*'s musical guest and the star of "The Creep," an *SNL* Digital Short video film featuring a nerdy dance floor move. Cult filmmaker John Waters appears at the beginning of the video to introduce the short.

as Andy Samberg, Jorma Taccone, Akiva Schaffer, Bill Hader, Chris Parnell, Kristen Wiig, and Kenan Thompson. The shorts also feature performances by famous Hollywood stars such as Jon Hamm, Justin Timberlake, Neil Patrick Harris, Nicki Minaj, Pee-wee Herman, Akon, and director Steven Spielberg. But that's not *SNL*'s only move toward the digital space. Sketches that make it to dress rehearsal but that are eventually cut from the show can sometimes be seen online (on the NBC.com site) as bonus content.

In a series of sketches in election year 2008, Tina Fey *(left)* had enormous success spoofing that year's Republican vice presidential candidate, Alaska governor Sarah Palin. Amy Poehler *(right)* sometimes joined her, playing one of that year's Democratic presidential contenders, Hillary Rodham Clinton. Fey's characterization of Palin is iconic *SNL* political satire.

CHAPTER 2
DIVERSITY...
"YEAH, THAT'S THE TICKET!"

SATURDAY NIGHT LIVE HAS BEEN A LEADER in bringing gender balance and racial diversity to American television and comedy.   Over the years, a growing number of writers, producers, and performers on the show have reflected this diversity. For example, writer-performer Tina Fey swiftly rose up the ranks of *SNL* during her nine seasons on the show (1997–2006). She eventually became the show's first female head writer (in 1999) as well as the coanchor of *SNL*'s "Weekend Update" news parody segment the following year.

TINA'S CONTRIBUTION

When Fey was supervising *SNL*'s writing staff, the show's sketches tackled just about every topic under the sun. They also pointedly took on issues specific to women's experience. For example, the "Mom's Jeans" sketch was a fake commercial (penned by Fey) that advertises a product, cinched at the waist, to make women look like stereotypically asexual moms. After Fey left the show in 2006, she still occasionally made a guest appearance. When she did, her sketches sometimes looked at gender-related issues, such as the challenges faced by female politicians. For example, one 2008 sketch, titled "A Nonpartisan Message from Governor Sarah Palin & Senator Hillary Clinton," involved Alaskan governor Sarah Palin (played by Fey) and New York senator Hillary Rodham Clinton (played by Amy Poehler). In September 2008, when the sketch aired, Governor Palin was the Republican vice presidential nominee and Senator Clinton was a former contender for the Democratic presidential nomination. In the "Nonpartisan Message" sketch, Palin and Clinton scold the media for relying on sexist stereotyping to describe them. Fey (as Palin) says, "So please, stop photoshopping my head on sexy bikini pictures!" Poehler (as Clinton) adds: "And stop saying I have 'cankles'!" The sketch mocked the way the press focused on Palin's and Clinton's looks, rather than on their skills and accomplishments.

Fey's probing commentary was fresh and insightful—and groundbreaking. In a 2008 *Vanity Fair* article about women in comedy, TV critic Alessandra Stanley commented on the ways in which Fey changed the show: "Suddenly, *S.N.L.* sketches were written by women, for women; the biggest stars were [Amy] Poehler and Maya Rudolph; and the [*SNL*] oh-God-I-hate-myself-so-much routines [about women] seemed passé."

WHEN AMY MET TINA

Tina Fey worked exceptionally well with Amy Poehler. The two met in 1993 in a class at Chicago's ImprovOlympic (now known as iO) Theater. Charna Halpern, cofounder of iO, remarks that Fey and Poehler were "just instantly brilliant. . . . They were not the typical women who get steamrolled by men. [They] were no shrinking violets. They were bold and ballsy and fearless."

The two remained friends after Fey was cast on *Saturday Night Live*. When Poehler joined the show in 2001, they were both ecstatic. As Fey recalled in her book *Bossypants*, "I was so happy. Weirdly, I remember thinking, 'My friend is here! My friend is here!' Even though things had been going great for me at the show, with Amy there, I felt less alone." Fey and Poehler became the first female coanchors of "Weekend Update" in September 2004. Previously, the segment had been anchored by a man, a woman, or one coanchor of each gender but never by two women.

Amy Poehler was great on her own too. She proved she was a comedic dynamo, with hyperactive characters such as the chatterbox child Kaitlin or the one-legged reality show contestant Amber. As Amber proudly describes herself in one sketch, "My name's Amber, I got hepatitis B, a mad case of bedbugs, and I'm rocking one leg." Audiences responded enthusiastically to the energy of Poehler's manic, excitable, and enthusiastic *SNL* characters.

For the past couple of decades, female writers such as Paula Pell, Emily Spivey, and Marika Sawyer have also been an influential part of the show. So was Beth McCarthy-Miller, director of the show from 1995 until 2006. Of the four directors to helm *SNL* since 1975, she has been the only female director. Comic performers Maya Rudolph, Kristen Wiig, and Nasim Pedrad have all created memorable roles. Rudolph does a hilariously insane impression of fashion designer Donatella Versace. Wiig's character Shanna is the seductive and sexy object of desire for every man in sight—until she spits food or passes gas. Pedrad's Tippy character is a spoof of the socially awkward person you sometimes meet at parties, who interrupts other people's conversations

Legendary actor Robert De Niro *(left)* impersonated the flamboyant entertainer-illusionist Roy Horn (of the duo Siegfried and Roy), with Maya Rudolph *(right)* in a classic take on high-fashion designer Donatella Versace. Their December 2002 *SNL* skit was known as "A Very Versace Chanukah."

in order to be in on a joke. Like Amy Poehler's Kaitlin character, Tippy is a classic example of an *SNL* performer using the show as a forum to make pointed observations about the awkward misfits we encounter in everyday life.

BREAKING NEW GROUND

In recent years, women aren't the only ones breaking ground on *SNL*. The voices of a cast of racially diverse performers have also grown more prominent. Jay Pharoah, who is African American, does spot-on impressions of black celebrities such as President Barack Obama and actor Denzel Washington. Pharoah's Obama impression is layered and fascinating, containing the stilted pauses, unique physical mannerisms, and other eccentricities that characterize an Obama speech. Pharoah's Denzel Washington impression is a wry commentary on the actor's fondness for chewing the scenery, or overacting. Like many actors, Denzel Washington is in love with himself and the sound of his own voice. He's a ham, and Jay Pharoah plays him that way. The impression works because it's accurate, because it's closely observed, and because it treats Washington not as a black actor but as an actor.

Host Kerry Washington (*left*) parodies media mogul Oprah Winfrey alongside Jay Pharoah's impersonation of President Obama in a sketch in November 2013. The sketch highlighted the lack of African American females in the *SNL* cast.

    SNL's diverse cast also includes Kenan Thompson, who plays DeAndre Cole, the obnoxious, interruption-prone host of the fictional BET (Black Entertainment Television) talk show "What Up with That?" Maya Rudolph played the love-struck, geeky preteen Megan in the "Wake Up, Wakefield" sketches set in Wakefield Middle School. Fred Armisen, of Venezuelan heritage, played cheesy Venezuelan nightclub comedian Fericito. Horatio Sanz played children's book illustrator Jasper Hahn, whose illustrations always started out as drawings of genitals . . . and ended up as harmless drawings of animals.

BACK IN THE DAY

But it wasn't always this way. In the 1970s and the 1980s, *Saturday Night Live* was more of a boy's club. It was much harder for women and people of color to get good, prominent roles on the show. Gilda Radner was the lone female cast member to shine as a solo performer in the show's original lineup. By contrast, Jane Curtin and Laraine Newman were both funny in ensemble pieces such as the Coneheads sketches. However, neither Curtin nor Newman carried any of the memorable early sketches by themselves.

    Similarly, with the exception of Eddie Murphy, African American performers on *SNL* were usually underutilized in the early years of the show. This was true for black performers such as Danitra Vance, Damon Wayans, Jerry Minor, Finesse Mitchell, Dean Edwards, and Garrett Morris. One of Morris's most famous roles was in the "Headmaster for the New York School for the Hard of Hearing" sketch, a recurring "Weekend Update" feature in which he would shout out the headlines. (At the time, television did not offer closed-captioning text for deaf viewers and instead provided sign language interpreters in a video inset in the corner of the screen.) Morris also provided all the impersonations of black celebrities, such as Louis Armstrong and James Brown. All the same, Morris and other early *SNL* black performers never rose to the same levels of popularity and prominence on the show as their white colleagues. As Benjamin Svetkey pointed out in *Entertainment Weekly,* "[Garret Morris] was more often given bits involving racial stereotypes, like the infamous 'Tarbrush' sketch, an ad parody for a toothpaste that dulled African Americans' supposedly too-shiny teeth. (The bit got pulled—mercifully—at the last minute.)"

AND THEN CAME CHRIS ROCK

When Chris Rock joined the show in 1990, he became good friends with Adam Sandler, David Spade, and Chris Farley. Yet Rock felt that *SNL* in the 1990s was not a place where a black performer had a chance to thrive. Rock has said that "with [fellow African American cast member] Tim Meadows being on the show, you know somewhere in your mind that if there's two nonwhite, pretty good sketches, they probably won't both get on. . . . You're never going to see this sketch with a bunch of black people, and this other sketch with a bunch of black people, back-to-back." Tim Meadows agrees with Rock's assessment, pointing out that he was never in more than four sketches per episode during the nine years he was on *SNL*. He points out that even as a veteran player, he had less exposure than did white performers on the show. He remembers that "even when Jimmy [Fallon] was a featured player [a new cast member], he had more sketches than I would."

SNL did launch many black performers into larger careers. Garrett Morris, for example, became a notable TV character actor. He played a recurring character or was a member of the main cast on such beloved shows as *Hunter* (1984–1991), *Roc* (1991–1994), *Martin* (1992–1997), *The Jamie Foxx Show* (1996–2001), and the hit sitcom *2 Broke Girls*, which launched in 2011. Chris Rock went on to host his own acclaimed late-night

In the 1990s, Chris Rock played Nat X, the politically militant host of a fictional talk show called "The Dark Side," in which the confrontational character took on highly charged racial issues with his guests. Rock used much of his original stand-up material in the sketches.

comedy show and became a movie star, author, and famed stand-up comic. Tim Meadows would become a well-known supporting actor in films such as *Mean Girls* (2004), *Walk Hard: The Dewey Cox Story* (2007), and *Jack and Jill* (2011). And Damon Wayans was one of the founders of the legendary TV sketch series *In Living Color* (1990–1994), before starring in the sitcom *My Wife and Kids* (2001–2005).

Tracy Morgan Joins the Show

Tracy Morgan joined the *SNL* cast in 1996. Early on, Morgan appeared in a sketch in which he introduced himself to the audience by reminding them that they had previously seen him only in the background in other *SNL* sketches. However, Morgan soon created characters who demanded the spotlight. They include the effeminate, easily enraged TV show host Brian Fellow and the oversexed space explorer Astronaut Jones *(pictured right)*. Morgan's characters—and the sketches in which they appear—are so layered and unpredictable that they avoid racial clichés and stereotyping.

Tracy Morgan's comedy persona—the crazy, anything-goes loose cannon—isn't one that the audience associates with a performer of any specific race. By being bolder, more unpredictable, crazier, and louder than his colleagues, Tracy Morgan demanded that the audience pay attention to him. Earlier *SNL* greats such as Chris Farley and John Belushi, the show's previous "wild men," rose to prominence through similar comedic strengths.

FROM NANCY REAGAN TO JODIE FOSTER

SNL has had quite a few gay writers, such as Paula Pell and James Anderson, over the years. Yet the show has featured very few openly gay cast members. Terry Sweeney, on the show during the 1985–1986 season, was the first. In fact, according to *People* magazine, Sweeney was the first openly gay performer on American network television. In 1986 Sweeney told *People* that he was openly gay because "no one else in entertainment was saying [that they were gay]. . . . I was tired of invisibility. I wanted people to know gay people are normal with regular jobs and careers like everybody else." This was a groundbreaking sentiment, coming at a time when many gay show business performers were in the closet. Sweeney's most famous character on *SNL* was his dead-on impersonation of then First Lady Nancy Reagan. Reagan's son Ron remarked that Sweeney was more like his mom than his actual mom.

Kate McKinnon is the first out lesbian in the *SNL* cast. Before joining the show in 2012, she was on the LGBT-themed sketch comedy program *The Big Gay Sketch Show* (2007–2010), which aired on Logo Network. At *Saturday Night Live,* McKinnon has done impressions of famous lesbian celebrities, such as *Glee* star Jane Lynch and legendary actor-director Jodie Foster. In a January 2013 episode, McKinnon famously parodied Foster's rambling, jittery Golden Globe Awards acceptance speech from earlier that month, in which the famed actor mentioned "coming out." Although Foster had already come out publicly in 2007 at a *Hollywood Reporter* breakfast, many viewers saw the Golden Globes speech as the first

Kate McKinnon, the first out lesbian actor on *SNL*, portrays Jodie Foster in a parody of her Golden Globes acceptance speech of 2013.

public announcement of Foster's sexuality. McKinnon used the *SNL* sketch to parody Foster's nervousness and her seeming reluctance to come out of the closet. McKinnon (as Foster) says, "I am . . . gayyyyyme for anything. I'm just totally game for anything. . . . Also, I am officially a Lesssslie Neilsen fan." She almost comes out a couple other times, before finally declaring, "So whew, it's all finally out there. That is such a giant weight off of my lesbian chest."

"NEW YORK'S HOTTEST CLUB IS . . ."

One of the most popular examples of gay *SNL* characters is the Ambiguously Gay Duo. Veteran *SNL* writer Robert Smigel created this long-running series of animated shorts about Ace and Gary (voiced by comedians Stephen Colbert and Steve Carell, respectively), two superheroes whose dialogue is filled with sexual innuendo. As Ace and Gary face off against supervillains, those same bad guys get sidetracked, debating whether Ace and Gary are gay. This was Smigel's sly commentary on the media's obsession over which celebrities are secretly gay. "The Ambiguously Gay Duo" shorts originally aired on

Short on Content, Long on Talent

The "Ambiguously Gay Duo" shorts are part of a long tradition. Actor and comedian Albert Brooks, best known for his performances in movies such as *Taxi Driver* (1976), *Broadcast News* (1987), *Out of Sight* (1998), and *Finding Nemo* (2003), directed and starred in six short films for the first season of *Saturday Night Live* (1975–1976). Talented writers, directors, and performers—such as Walter Williams, Tom Schiller, Gary Weis, Eddie Murphy, Andy Samberg, Kristen Wiig, and Jay Pharoah—followed suit, creating quirky short films for *SNL*.

Penelope Spheeris was the producer of the original Albert Brooks *SNL* short films. She went on to direct the hit movie *Wayne's World* (1992), based on the *Saturday Night Live* "Wayne's World" sketches starring Mike Myers and Dana Carvey.

the short-lived sketch comedy series *The Dana Carvey Show* in 1996. Later that same year, when the show was canceled, the duo moved over to *SNL*, where they have remained ever since. In a recent 2011 "Ambiguously Gay Duo" short (filmed partially in live-action), Jon Hamm and Jimmy Fallon played real life versions of Ace and Gary.

Then there's Stefon, the drug-addled gay club kid played by Bill Hader from 2008 to 2013. Stefon usually appeared on *SNL*'s "Weekend Update" segment. "Update" anchor Seth Meyers would introduce him as a city correspondent, who could recommend New York events and destinations for tourists and other visitors. Stefon's recommendations are always bizarre parties and unusual nightclubs filled with oddball characters such as Germfs (German Smurfs), DJ Baby Bok Choy, and Jewish Dracula Sidney Applebaum. Stefon often starts out his nightlife recommendation with "New York's hottest club is . . ." and then mentions the name of a club with a sexually suggestive name such as Crease, Spicy, or Push. Stefon's character has a huge crush on Seth Meyers. Meyers's anchor character is immune to Stefon's charms until

As club kid Stefon, Bill Hader *(left)* gave a pitch-perfect impression of the hip, New York, gay club crowd. "Weekend Update" host Seth Meyers *(right)* was usually unable to withhold laughter at Stefon's spirited, somewhat neurotic delivery. In Stefon's final appearance on "Update," the two get married.

the final "Stefon" sketch (May 18, 2013), in which Stefon and Meyers are married. Hader's Stefon was popular, and the performer remarked that when he was on *SNL*, he was frequently approached by fans who said they knew someone just like Stefon.

LOOKING AHEAD

Saturday Night Live has been under fire more recently for not doing more to expand the diversity of its cast. For example, the show has never hired an Asian cast member, and in its on-air history, *SNL* has had only four black female cast members: Yvonne Hudson (1980–1981), Danitra Vance (1985–1986), Ellen Cleghorne (1991–1995), and Maya Rudolph (2000–2007). Only three of those performers were repertory players (members of the main cast). Hudson was a featured player and was fired in the middle of the season. In a September 2013 interview with *theGrio*—a website with content focused on African Americans—Jay Pharoah said that *SNL* should cast a black woman on the show. "They need to pay attention," he commented. Many other publications, both online and print, echoed this sentiment.

To address the issue directly, the November 3, 2013, episode of *Saturday Night Live* featured a cold open in which the host, actor Kerry Washington, played both First Lady Michelle Obama and mega-celebrity talk show host Oprah Winfrey. Washington makes a superfast costume change to go between the two characters, and a message from the show's producers appears on-screen during the sketch:

> *The producers of* Saturday Night Live *would like to apologize to Kerry Washington for the number of black women she will be asked to play tonight. . . . [This is partially] because* SNL *does not currently have a black woman in the cast. . . . [We] agree this is not an ideal situation and look forward to rectifying it in the near future . . . unless, of course, we fall in love with another white guy first.*

The message was clear: *SNL* knew that it needed to work on diversifying its cast. In December 2013, *SNL* announced that it had begun auditioning to add a new black female cast member to the show. And in January 2014, African American female comedian Sasheer Zamata joined the cast.

Chevy Chase is forever linked to his bumbling impersonation of President Gerald Ford, here surrounded by Garrett Morris (far left) and John Belushi (right) as Secret Service agents. Actor Buck Henry (behind Chase), a frequent SNL host, played Ford's press secretary Ron Nessen in this January 1976 "Oval Office" sketch.

CHAPTER 3
LIVE FROM NEW YORK, IT'S ... POLITICS?

SATURDAY NIGHT LIVE'S HUMOR HAS ALWAYS BEEN EDGY. This means that the *SNL* writers and performers are never afraid to comment on politics. In fact, political satire has always been one of the show's strengths, from Chevy Chase's slapstick impression of President Gerald Ford in the 1970s to Tina Fey's 2008 caricatures of vice presidential candidate Sarah Palin. Both impressions are ingrained in the public consciousness. When many people think of Gerald Ford, they still think of Chevy Chase stumbling and dropping things in his spoof of the physically clumsy president. Similarly, when people think of Sarah Palin, they often think of Tina Fey in her look-alike hairdo, making fun of Palin's gaffes.

But have *SNL's* sketches affected real-life political careers? Does the show wield that much power? Sometimes it does.

THE "DOOFUS IN CHIEF"

Decades before Gerald Ford was president of the United States, he was a star football player at the University of Michigan. In later years, he was a skilled golfer. By many accounts, he was a graceful athlete, a model of agility and control. So why do so many people remember him as a clumsy doofus?

In a notoriously embarrassing moment as president, Ford took a spectacular tumble down the stairs of Air Force One (the president's personal airplane) on a trip to Austria in 1975. Chevy Chase turned that goof into a weekly joke on *Saturday Night Live* during the show's first season. In his Gerald Ford sketches on the show, Chase made no attempt to look or sound like Ford. However, through good writing and Chase's mastery of slapstick, he was able to stretch the "Ford is clumsy" jokes to their most absurd and surreal extreme. In one sketch, Chase's President Ford uses his necktie to wipe his nose after a sneeze; he mistakes a glass of water for a telephone; he bumps his forehead on his own desk; and finally, he falls over his own desk.

Chase's caricatures of Ford changed the image of the president in the eyes of the public. As one commentator later noted, "Chevy Chase's sketches rebranded the president, and might have influenced the [1976 presidential] elections by instilling in people's minds an image of an inept president [that voters would not want to elect back into office]. The moment launched Chevy's career, but was a thorn in Ford's side for the rest of his life."

"Chevy Chase's sketches rebranded the president, and might have influenced the [1976 presidential] elections by instilling in people's minds an image of an inept president."

All the same, Gerald Ford liked Chevy Chase's *SNL* sketches so much that the two eventually met and became friends. In January 2007, shortly after Ford's death, Chase reflected on his unlikely friendship with the former president. Open about his own history of drug addiction, Chase mentioned that he and Ford were forever linked with each other, not just because of the *SNL* sketches but because of a shared connection with addiction. Chase pointed out, "If it hadn't been for the courage of Mr. Ford's wife, Betty, for admitting [in 1978] to [her] alcohol problem, I would never have received the help I needed in the early 1980s at the Betty Ford clinic [founded in 1982 by Ford herself], located not far from the Ford residence near Palm Springs [California].”

Chase has also fondly remembered the ease with which Ford accepted the *SNL* mockery. He points to a lunch with the Fords in the late 1980s (after Ford was no longer president) as a prime example. Chase; his wife, Jayni; and the Fords were watching actors’ screen tests from a forthcoming movie about Betty Ford. Chase suggested that the two men help their wives, who were trying to get the video to work. Ford said, “No, no, Chevy. Don’t even think about it. I’ll probably get electrocuted, and you’ll be picked up and arrested for murder.”

FEY’S ACCOLADES LEAD TO PALIN’S FAILIN’

In the show’s 2008–2009 season premiere, Tina Fey was brought back specifically to play Alaskan governor and then Republican vice presidential candidate Sarah Palin. Fey returned on several occasions to do more “Sarah Palin” sketches, which were fantastically popular. Palin seemed to like Tina Fey’s impression and laughed about it publicly. For example, in September 2008, Palin gave two widely mocked interviews with CBS’s Katie Couric. Palin came across as woefully unprepared for the interviews and ill-informed on issues. At a Florida campaign rally the next month, she made light of the interviews by joking, “I was just trying to keep Tina Fey in business, just giving her some information.” (The Katie Couric interviews were later parodied on *SNL* in a sketch with Fey as Palin and Poehler as Couric. Fey has said that she used some of Palin’s responses word for word in the sketch.)

LIVE FROM NEW YORK, IT’S SARAH PALIN!

Fey’s impersonation of Sarah Palin led to Palin herself appearing on *SNL,* despite being routinely parodied on the show. In a sketch early in the 2008–2009 season, the camera went backstage, revealing Palin and Lorne Michaels standing together, watching a Tina Fey sketch *about* Palin (it was a sketch within a sketch). Actor (and frequent *SNL* host) Alec Baldwin showed up and began to talk to Palin, thinking she was actually Tina Fey. The encounter was obviously scripted, but it still generated media buzz. Baldwin—known for his support of liberal

Democratic candidates—had nothing but praise for the way Palin "came on [the show] to be a good sport." Later that same season, Palin appeared in a "Weekend Update" skit in October 2008. Sitting next to "Update" coanchor Seth Meyers, the two rocked out as Amy Poehler delivered a rap tune mocking Palin.

The show did appear to have a negative impact on Palin's political career. For example, the *Washington Times* reported on two polls that found that the McCain-Palin ticket had lost ground among independent voters, whose support the team would need to win the presidential race. The polling indicated that Tina Fey's impression of Sarah Palin was playing a role in those voters' decision not to back the ticket. As reporter David R. Sands explained, "Thirty-three percent of independents said [the] 'Tina Fey effect' is hurting the McCain-Palin ticket, compared to 9 percent who said it was helpful."

The real Republican vice presidential candidate of 2008, Sarah Palin, rocked out with Amy Poehler and Seth Meyers during a "Weekend Update" skit in October 2008. Palin was the frequent butt of jokes on *SNL* that year.

BUSH, BUBBA, BUSH II, AND BARACK

Other *SNL* cast members have done impressions of major politicians, and some have come close to matching the impact of Fey's Palin impression and of Chase's Ford impression. In the twenty-first century, Fred Armisen's and Jay Pharoah's impressions of President Barack Obama are critically acclaimed for their accuracy. Among the strongest in earlier shows have been Dana Carvey's impressions of President George H. W. Bush in the late 1980s and the early 1990s and Will Ferrell's impressions of President George W. Bush (in office from 2001 until 2009).

Dana Carvey took great pains to look and sound as much like George H. W. Bush as possible, and he pulled off an astoundingly accurate impression. For example, when imitating the president, Carvey would often say that he wasn't going to be intimidated by his opponents. Then he would say, for emphasis, "Not gonna do it! Not gonna do it!" This was a parody of the president's attempt to come across as firm and tough, to overcome the perception that he was somewhat timid. Bush was so tickled by Carvey's impressions that he invited him to the White House in December 1992. There he performed that very same impression for an audience made up of the president, the First Lady, and members of the White House staff.

Fred Armisen *(far right)* perfectly captured President Barack Obama's steady yet somewhat choppy style of speech. Here, he and Jason Sudeikis as Vice President Joe Biden lampoon the nation's leaders shortly after Obama's inauguration in January 2009.

Before It Goes Live

How exactly is an episode of *Saturday Night Live* put together? It goes something like this: On Monday, ideas for sketches are first pitched in rough form to the guest host. On Tuesday, the writers work nonstop all day and late into the night writing sketches. Then on Wednesday, the show first starts to take shape. During a big meeting, writers and cast members read through all the sketch ideas. On average, approximately thirty-five to forty sketches will be on the table. Of those, eleven or twelve will get the final go-ahead.

On Thursday is a massive rewrite session. The writers revise their sketches, and rough sketches are turned into final drafts. On Friday is a rehearsal. And on Saturday, before the actual show is taped, there's a dress rehearsal before a live studio audience, with all the performers in costume. Even sketches that have made it this far can be cut at the last minute. Out of the eleven or twelve sketches that may still be in the show at this point, another three or four might get cut after dress rehearsal. On average, eight to twelve sketches make it to air each Saturday night. (This does not include other content, such as the opening monologue, two musical numbers, the "Weekend Update" segment, parody commercials, and short films.) At eleven thirty eastern time, the show goes live.

Gilda Radner *(left)* with *SNL* writer Marilyn Suzanne Miller in New York in 1978

Will Ferrell's later impressions of President George W. Bush were hilarious, mostly for the way Ferrell mocked Bush as childlike and dim-witted. (Bush was famously known for a lack of polish and sophistication in his public speeches.) In a 2008 interview, Ferrell said he had no idea how Bush felt about an impersonation in which Ferrell mispronounced *strategy* as "strategerie," among many other mix-ups. This was a play on the real Bush's well-known tendency to mispronounce words. Ferrell explained, "You know, there was that stuff written about how the [Bush] staff loved 'strategerie,' and how he called them 'strategerie meetings.' I had a couple of opportunities to go and meet him, and I declined, partly out of comedic purposes, because when I was on the show [*Saturday Night Live*] at the time, it didn't make sense to really meet the people that you play, for fear of them influencing you."

Will Ferrell captured President George W. Bush's awkward delivery and vocabulary trip-ups to humorous effect.

" . . . GOOD NIGHT, AND HAVE A PLEASANT TOMORROW"

On the political front, *SNL* has also made viewers laugh with the "Weekend Update" segment. In fact, "Weekend Update" is the only part of the show—other than the cold open with its "Live from New York, It's Saturday Night" ending—that has been a part of *SNL* from the first episode.

SNL "Weekend Update" host Jane Curtin was often paired with loser featured guests on the mock news segment. Here, she expresses her disgust at a sleeping Bill Murray in a December 1977 installment of "Update."

"Weekend Update" is a mock news segment that makes fun of the evening news and current events. With Chevy Chase as its first anchor, "Weekend Update" was a direct parody of the buttoned-down, humorless demeanor of most evening television news anchors. In the mid-1990s, Chevy Chase talked about what inspired him to create the "Weekend Update" segment:

> The thought behind it, thematically, was, "Here's an
> opportunity to do parody, to be funny as a newsman, and to
> have a phone—which they all seemed to have at the time—and
> use that as a vehicle for satire to say damn well what I want on
> the news.

Straight parody of the evening news went out the window in 2000, when Jimmy Fallon and Tina Fey became coanchors of "Weekend Update." At that point, the segment shifted its approach. As Tom Shales and James Andrew Miller wrote about Fallon and Fey in the 2002 book *Live from New York,* "It's no longer a parody of the actual newscast; now it's just a sexy pair of smart alecks sitting around and making fun of the world." This is also true for the "Update" years of coanchors Tina Fey and Amy Poehler (2004–2006), coanchors Amy Poehler and Seth Meyers (2006–2008), solo anchor Seth Meyers (2008–2013), and coanchors Seth Meyers and Cecily Strong (2013). With each anchor (or pair of anchors), "Weekend Update" is like watching your coolest friends make clever, witty jokes about current events. But one thing about "Weekend Update" has remained constant: the steady stream of topical, edgy jokes mocking the headlines of the day.

Kristen Wiig *(center)* as Dooneese Maharelle is surrounded by *(left to right)* Nasim Pedrad, Bobby Moynihan, Kate McKinnon, and Taran Killam in a December 2013 *SNL* skit spoofing NBC's live musical version of *The Sound of Music.*

CHAPTER 4

I'M KRISTEN WIIG, AND YOU'RE NOT!

SATURDAY NIGHT LIVE IS A STAR-MAKING MACHINE. It is responsible for the creation of more major movie and TV stars than any other single TV show of the late twentieth century.

FEARLESS TWENTY-FIRST-CENTURY CELEBS

Kristen Wiig

When she was on *Saturday Night Live* (2005–2012), Kristen Wiig's nickname might as well have been "Fearless." She was unafraid of making herself look as creepy and bizarre as possible. Yet somehow you always wanted to know more about her characters. For example, who but Kristen Wiig would come up with—and get away with— Dooneese Maharelle, one of the four singing Maharelle sisters on *SNL*'s spoof of the cheesy *Lawrence Welk Show* (1951–1982)? Everything about that character—the tiny plastic baby doll hands, the oversized Klingon-style forehead, the off-key Minnie Mouse voice—is deranged and almost revolting. Yet audiences clamored for more. In Wiig's hands, the character isn't just revolting, she's *fascinatingly* revolting and therefore endearing.

Wiig took her knack for unusual, anything-goes characterizations to the world of film, cowriting and starring in the Oscar-nominated 2011 movie *Bridesmaids.* Her character in that film, Annie, faces a series of setbacks and disasters. In the movie, as in her *SNL* sketches, Wiig proves that she understands how to create a character who represents a mix of tragedy and comedy.

Amy Poehler

Like many *Saturday Night Live* performers, Amy Poehler prepared for a life in comedy by training at Second City, the prestigious improvisational theater in Chicago. Soon, Poehler became part of a Chicago-based sketch comedy troupe called the Upright Citizens Brigade (UCB). With UCB she moved to New York City in 1996. Two years later, UCB got a show of its own (also called *Upright Citizens Brigade*) on Comedy Central. The TV series was canceled in 2000. The following year, Poehler was cast on *Saturday Night Live,* where she remained through 2008. She's one of very few performers in *SNL*'s history to make the jump from featured player to full-fledged cast member in the middle of her first season. (Most cast members have to wait at least one full season to make that transition.) During her years on *SNL* and after, Poehler has always specialized in playing characters with high levels of energy and an unflagging sense of enthusiasm.

Nowhere is this more evident than in her starring role on the hit NBC series *Parks and Recreation,* which premiered in 2009. On that show, Poehler plays Leslie Knope, an endlessly perky bureaucrat living in the fictional town of Pawnee, Indiana. In her drive, ambition, and optimism, Leslie Knope is also similar to Bessie, the character Poehler voiced on the animated Nickelodeon series *The Mighty B!* (2008–2011), a show she cocreated. Bessie is an imaginative Honeybee scout (like a girl scout), who has earned more Bee Badges than any other Honeybee scout in history.

Like the Leslie Knope and Bessie characters, Poehler herself is known as a beacon of positive energy. As her *Parks and Recreation* costar Chris Pratt told MTV.com in 2009, "[Amy] continually goes out of her way to make everyone feel comfortable. . . . She has no ego [problems], but she's also a star."

Tina Fey

On *Saturday Night Live,* Tina Fey stands out not only for her Sarah Palin impersonations but also for her work on "Weekend Update," which she coanchored with Jimmy Fallon (2000–2004) and with Amy Poehler (2004–2006). Fey's comic persona and her writing for the show were smart, pointed, and edgy.

She brought those same qualities to the TV show *30 Rock* (2006–2013), a witty sitcom that she created for NBC and in which she starred. The sitcom is about Liz Lemon, the head writer of a fictional sketch comedy show, who struggles to deal with the neurotic stars of the show and the show's self-obsessed network executive, Jack Donaghy (played by Alec Baldwin). The sitcom was loosely inspired by Tina Fey's career at *SNL,* where she was the head writer at the show's headquarters within 30 Rockefeller Plaza (30 Rock) in New York City. *SNL* creator Lorne Michaels was also the executive producer of *30 Rock*, which brought *SNL* talent such as Tracy Morgan and Rachel Dratch to the show.

In *SNL*'s 2004–2005 season, Amy Poehler coanchored "Weekend Update" for the first time. Here, she hams it up with Tina Fey in a January 2005 segment.

Tina Fey has been incredibly active as a writer and a performer in a variety of media. She wrote the screenplay for the 2004 Lindsay Lohan movie *Mean Girls.* This insightful film takes a funny look at the ways in which teenage girls can verbally and psychologically undermine one another. Fey herself had a supporting role in the movie, alongside fellow *SNL* alums Tim Meadows and Amy Poehler.

In 2011 Fey authored the best-selling autobiographical book *Bossypants,* in which she comments on her life and career with deft humor and sarcasm. For example, in response to men who perpetuate the absurd claim that women are not funny, Fey writes, "My hat goes off to them. It is an impressively arrogant move to conclude that because *you* don't like something, it is empirically [based on direct observation] not good. I don't like Chinese food, but I don't write articles trying to prove it doesn't exist."

In addition to her work as an actor, TV writer, screenwriter, and author, Tina Fey is the winner of multiple awards. For her work as a writer on *SNL,* she has won an Emmy and two Writers Guild awards. In 2009 she won an Emmy for Guest Appearance by an Actress in a Comedy Series (for her impression of Sarah Palin on the 2008–2009 season of *Saturday Night Live*). And in 2010, she won the prestigious Mark Twain Prize for American Humor, cementing her status as one of the generation's great humorists.

Will Ferrell

On *Saturday Night Live,* Will Ferrell played President George W. Bush as a regular fella, a lovable oaf who reminded many Americans of their next-door neighbor, their boss, or the local high school gym teacher. Like Kristen Wiig, Ferrell excels in creating characters who are flawed yet likable and funny.

This is also true in Ferrell's film work. Characters such as Ron Burgundy, the protagonist of the *Anchorman* films (2004 and 2013), or Ricky Bobby, the lead role in *Talladega Nights: The Ballad of Ricky Bobby* (2006), use their outward charm and swagger to mask inner pain. Each movie is a story about a public figure and idol of millions, who— due to his own arrogance and unwillingness to listen to others—loses everything and has to claw his way back to the top. That's what makes these characters more than just fools. They learned something from their experiences that makes them better people.

NINETIES-ERA NOTABLES

Adam Sandler

Adam Sandler specialized in playing "man-child" characters, grown men who act like children. Sandler's variations on the man-child character included "Canteen Boy," a naive assistant scoutmaster who has, as Sandler himself once put it, "stayed in the Scouts too long."

After Sandler left *SNL* in 1995, his film career took off with the film *Billy Madison* (released that same year). His success as a movie star is based on the same qualities that made him such a big hit on *SNL*. He comes across as "one of the guys" and displays genuine warmth and sincerity in his performances. Audiences like him because they sense that his characters are good, kind people. For the most part, he seems to have these two definitive film personas:

With a comedy club and television background, Adam Sandler was hired as a writer for *SNL* in 1990. He quickly became a featured player known for goofy, yet pointed songs.

1) His "man-child" character, which he played in movies such as *Billy Madison, The Waterboy* (1998), and *That's My Boy* (2012).

2) His more mature, intelligent persona, which he played in romantic comedies such as *The Wedding Singer* (1998), *50 First Dates* (2004), and *Just Go with It* (2011). In these roles, Sandler is less a traditional romantic leading man and more like your cool older brother making movies instead of being away at college.

Like Tina Fey, Sandler is known for his loyalty to fellow comedians and comedy writers. Through his production company, Happy

Madison, he produces TV shows and movies. And in many of his Happy Madison productions, he frequently casts other *SNL* performers. For example, Sandler's fellow *SNL* castmate Rob Schneider has appeared in supporting roles in Happy Madison films such as *The Waterboy* and *Big Daddy* (1999).

Who's Happy?

Adam Sandler's Happy Madison production company has produced many films featuring former *SNL* cast members. They include the following:

- The two *Deuce Bigalow* movies (1999 and 2005), both of which star Rob Schneider
- *Joe Dirt* (2001), which stars David Spade
- *The Master of Disguise* (2002), starring Dana Carvey
- *You Don't Mess with the Zohan* (2008), starring Sandler and featuring Robert Smigel, Rob Schneider, Kevin Nealon, and Chris Rock in supporting roles
- *Grown Ups* (2010), starring Sandler, David Spade, Chris Rock, and Rob Schneider and featuring Maya Rudolph, Colin Quinn, Tim Meadows, and Norm Macdonald in supporting roles

Mike Myers

As a child, Mike Myers wanted to be in show business. When he was ten, he appeared in a TV commercial, opposite Gilda Radner, who played his mother. Myers quickly developed a crush on the charming and hilarious actress. Months later, he found out that Radner was on a new TV show called *Saturday Night Live.* He vowed to one day be on that show.

As an adult, he got his wish, appearing on *SNL* after one of the show's former cast members, Martin Short, recommended him to the show's executive producer, Lorne Michaels. Myers appeared on *SNL* from 1989 until 1995, creating such bizarrely original characters as Dieter, host of the German talk show *"Sprockets"* and Linda Richman, host of the daytime chat show *"Coffee Talk."* But the Mike Myers *SNL* character that stands above all others is Wayne Campbell of the

"Wayne's World" sketches. When Myers first told the other *SNL* writers about his idea for the sketch, they didn't think it was very funny. But "Wayne's World"—with its two comically unmotivated, metalhead friends—was so popular that it spun off into a hugely successful feature film in 1992 and another in 1993. Memorable catchphrases from the pair include "We're not worthy!" (which they scream when talking to their musical idols, such as the rock band Aerosmith) and "Schwing!" (which they shout—accompanied by a pelvic thrust—when they see an extremely attractive girl).

Mike Myers *(left)* as Wayne Campbell and Dana Carvey *(right)* as Garth Algar are the metalhead hosts of a cable-access show they produce from the basement of Wayne's parents' home. Obsessed with the rock band Aerosmith, the duo eventually got to jam with their idols on a popular *SNL* episode in February 1990.

After leaving *SNL*, Myers starred in (and wrote the screenplay for) a new movie, *Austin Powers: International Man of Mystery* (1997). The film was a parody of James Bond spy movies and spawned two sequels. Like many of his *SNL* colleagues, Mike Myers makes his characters work because they're relatable. As a 1960s guy stuck in the 1990s, Austin Powers is a stranger in a strange land. Because viewers themselves often feel like outcasts, the character is sympathetic.

Myers has continued to make other movies. For example, he voiced the title character in the *Shrek* animated movies (2001–present) about a grouchy ogre with a heart of gold. The 2007 film *Shrek the Third* featured Myers's fellow *SNL* alums Cheri Oteri (the voice of Sleeping Beauty), Amy Poehler (Snow White), and Maya Rudolph (Rapunzel).

Cinema Night Live

Saturday Night Live sketches and characters spawned a wide range of movies. Of these films, *The Blues Brothers* (1980) and *Wayne's World* (1992) were the most successful, bringing in many millions of dollars at the box office. In chronological order, the *SNL* movies are the following:

- *Mr. Mike's Mondo Video* (1979)
- *The Blues Brothers* (1980)
- *Mr. Bill's Real Life Adventures* (1986, TV movie)
- *Wayne's World* (1992)
- *Bob Roberts* (1992, based on a short film that guest host Tim Robbins shot for a 1986 episode of *SNL*)
- *Mr. Saturday Night* (1992, based on the "Buddy Young Jr." sketches, which Billy Crystal had first performed on *Saturday Night Live*)

- *Coneheads* (1993)
- *Wayne's World 2* (1993)
- *It's Pat* (1994)
- *Stuart Saves His Family* (1995)
- *Blues Brothers 2000* (1998)
- *A Night at the Roxbury* (1998)
- *Superstar* (1999)
- *The Ladies Man* (2000)
- *MacGruber* (2010)

EXCELLENT EIGHTIES ICONS

Eddie Murphy

No question: Eddie Murphy is one of the biggest box office stars ever to emerge from *Saturday Night Live*. Throughout the 1980s, his films *48 Hrs.* (1982), *Trading Places* (1983), *Beverly Hills Cop* (1984), and *Coming to America* (1988) were among the top moneymakers of the era. When Eddie Murphy first appeared on the scene, many critics compared him to Richard Pryor, who was daring and edgy, even a little scary. Murphy's edginess in *SNL* sketches such as "Velvet Jones"

Eddie Murphy was never afraid to push the limits in his comedy. In a 1984 holiday segment of *SNL*'s "Mr. Robinson's Neighborhood," Murphy's character gives a vocabulary lesson, using the letter *X*.

X-CON

(about a sleazy infomercial pitchman) took the form of raunchy sexual content. Velvet offered viewers books on how to be a prostitute. This type of content was fully on display in his early movies as well. Murphy has said that the source of much of his biting humor lies in his teen experience, when he and his brother were briefly in foster care in New York.

After a string of box office duds in the early 1990s, Murphy reinvented himself . . . as the king of family-oriented comedies. He starred in kid-friendly fare such as *The Nutty Professor* (1996), *Dr. Dolittle* (1998), and *Daddy Day Care* (2003). He's also voiced the "Donkey" character in all the *Shrek* animated family films. Ironically, the comedian who was once thought of as too raw for prime time has largely become a children's entertainer.

Billy Crystal

When Billy Crystal came to *Saturday Night Live* for the 1984–1985 season, he brought something different to the table. Crystal's "Fernando" sketches, centered on shallow European talk show host Fernando, were largely improvised. This was a big contrast to the fully scripted content of most other *SNL* sketches before or since.

In both his *SNL* work and his later film work, Billy Crystal is a mix of old-school and new-school comedy. As a Jewish comic, he is heavily influenced by Jewish comics of the 1950s and the 1960s such as Henny Youngman, Jackie Mason, and Woody Allen. Their acts were sprinkled with Yiddish expressions and accents. (Yiddish is a language that combines German, Polish, and Hebrew and is spoken by Jews in many parts of the world.) When doing his impression of legendary African American singer-actor Sammy Davis Jr. (who was Jewish) on *SNL*, Crystal would often have Sammy casually throwing out Yiddish terms such as "kvelling" (feeling proud and happy) and "shpilkes" (a state of impatience or agitation).

Crystal's films show the same touch. For example, in his role as Miracle Max in the 1987 film

"You look mahvelous!" was the supremely popular catchphrase of Billy Crystal's Fernando talk show character, based on Latin lover screen idol Fernando Lamas. Known as a notorious playboy, Lamas was a romantic film lead in movies of the 1940s and the 1950s.

The Princess Bride (which costars *SNL*'s Christopher Guest), Crystal plays Miracle Max as an old Jewish man. In *Analyze This* (1999), the character he plays is a twist on the stereotype of the neurotic Jewish therapist. In the film, Crystal's newest client is a mob boss, played by tough-guy actor Robert De Niro. This pairing of an old comic cliché (the Jewish therapist) with a slightly scary character (the mobster) put a fresh spin on American film comedy.

SUPREME SEVENTIES SUPERSTARS

Bill Murray

Bill Murray came to *SNL* in the fall of 1976 as a little-known comedic actor to replace Chevy Chase. Murray went on to a serious, critically acclaimed movie career. At *SNL* Murray was well known for his "Weekend Update" anchor role, where he played an antiauthority nonconformist who had little patience for stupidity. He also played Nick the obnoxious lounge singer, whose hilariously off-key renditions of familiar tunes such as the *Star Wars* theme made you cringe—and laugh.

In the late 1970s and the early 1980s, Murray was king of "slob comedies," movies such as *Meatballs* (1979), *Caddyshack* (1980), and *Stripes* (1981). All of these movies are raunchy ensemble pieces in which down-to-earth underdogs stick it to uptight authority figures. They were inspired—either directly or indirectly—by the success of 1978's *Animal House* movie, which proved that American movie audiences were ready for a no-holds-barred style of shocking, gross-out humor.

Murray was king of "slob comedies," . . . . raunchy ensemble pieces in which down-to-earth underdogs stick it to uptight authority figures.

Murray went on to star in comedies such as the *Ghostbusters* films (1984 and 1989), *Scrooged* (1988), and *Groundhog Day* (1993). These films were cleverer than the slob comedies, and they were also cross-genre movies, mixing comedy and fantasy. Beginning in the late 1990s, Murray began to take on dramatic roles in serious films such as *Hyde Park on Hudson* (2012) and *The Monuments Men* (2014). He has also played supporting roles in small independent films by art house directors, including Jim Jarmusch's *Coffee and Cigarettes* (2003) and Wes Anderson's *Moonrise Kingdom* (2012). Murray was nominated for an Oscar for his starring role in Sofia Coppola's drama *Lost in Translation* (2003). In an ironic twist, the ultimate antiestablishment performer had been embraced by the showbiz establishment.

John Belushi

In the 1950s, actor James Dean starred in only three movies before dying tragically young in a car crash. John Belushi is the James Dean of *Saturday Night Live,* a rebellious, reckless wild man who lived fast and died young. Belushi died of a drug overdose in 1982, leading some of his showbiz colleagues to quit using drugs.

Like James Dean, who made his mark in a very brief career, John Belushi left a limited legacy too. It includes his work on *SNL* (1975–1979) and his acting work in two films, *National Lampoon's Animal House* (1978) and *The Blues Brothers* (1980). Before he died, Belushi did make several other movies, such as *Continental Divide* and *Neighbors*—both in 1981—but they died a quick death at the box office and few people have seen them.

Belushi is remembered for his two most famous movies and for his "average Joe" charm, which was at the heart of so many of his *SNL* bits. For example, the "Olympia Cafe" sketches focus on a busy Greek diner in which the owner, Pete (Belushi) had—it seemed—only one thing on the menu. And he yelled it out in each sketch: "Cheeseburger! Cheeseburger! Cheeseburger!" Belushi loved playing these types of blue-collar characters because that's who he was, and that's who he celebrated in his life and art.

Chevy Chase

Chevy Chase was *SNL*'s first real star, largely because he was handsome and charismatic; he didn't take anything too seriously; and he said his own name as often as possible while

Chevy Chase in the summer of 1976

on the show. His big catchphrase was "I'm Chevy Chase, and you're not!"

Chase admits that he left the show too soon—at the beginning of the second season in October 1976. After leaving *SNL,* Chase starred in the hit comedy *Foul Play* (1978), followed by a supporting role in *Caddyshack* (1980), and four *National Lampoon's Vacation* movies (1983, 1985, 1989, and 1997). In these films, Chase perfected the sarcastic, insincere, cocky persona he had developed in the "Weekend Update" segment on *SNL.*

Chase made a return to television, playing the character of aging tycoon Pierce Hawthorne in the NBC sitcom *Community,* which debuted in 2009. The *Community* gig was Chase's highest-profile role in many years, and his fans were happy to see him back on top.

Jane Curtin

Jane Curtin was usually cast as the "straight man" in many *SNL* sketches, playing straightlaced, prim characters driven to distraction by the outrageous oddballs played by John Belushi, Chevy Chase, or Bill Murray. She sometimes played outrageous oddballs herself, such as Enid Loopner, nerdy mother of the equally nerdy Lisa Loopner (played by Gilda Radner). Curtin was the solo anchor of "Weekend Update" in 1976–1977 (its first female anchor), coanchor with Dan Aykroyd in 1977–1978, and coanchor with Bill Murray from 1978 to 1980.

Curtin didn't always have the splashiest roles on *SNL,* but her work on that show proved that she was a dynamic actor with incredible range. She has used that range to build a long-lasting career as a TV star. For example, after leaving *SNL* in 1980, she starred in two very successful television sitcoms, *Kate & Allie* (1984–1989) and *Third Rock from the Sun* (1996–2001). She also played a supporting role in the three *Librarian* TV movies (2004, 2006, and 2008). She then went on to play the outspoken medical examiner Dr. Joanne Webster on the CBS police procedural drama *Unforgettable* (2011–present), starring Poppy Montgomery.

THANKS TO THE CAST AND CREW

Saturday Night Live began as one man's radical new idea. Lorne Michaels aimed to create a TV sketch comedy show that was in tune with the thoughts and feelings of young people and with the hot issues of the day. It was the first "rock & roll" comedy show, with an attitude of antiauthority rebelliousness.

Since then it has become much more. *Saturday Night Live* made comedy cool. Thanks to *SNL*, most major colleges have at least one resident sketch troupe, made up of teens and twenty-somethings hoping to be the next Andy Samberg or Kristen Wiig. S*aturday Night Live* also gave other TV sketch comedy shows permission to be subversive, daring, and edgy. Without the example set by *SNL,* none of the following sketch comedy shows would exist: *In Living Color* (1990–1994), *The Kids in the Hall* (1988–1995, also produced by Lorne Michaels), *Mr. Show with Bob and David* (1995–1998), *MADtv* (1995–2009), *The Chris Rock Show* (1997–2000), *Chappelle's Show* (2003–2006), *Robot Chicken* (2005–present), and *Key and Peele* (2012–present).

The pioneering "Weekend Update" mock news segment set the stage for other mock news shows such as *The Daily Show* (1996–present), *The Colbert Report* (2005–present), and *Nikki & Sara Live!* (2013–present). Many young Americans get their news from these mock news shows rather than from newspapers or mainstream network TV news, a trend that started with "Weekend Update" long ago.

In the end, *Saturday Night Live* affects how we view politics, how we think about celebrities, and how other TV sketch comedy shows approach their material. It has served as a celebrity factory, launching superstars such as Tina Fey, Kristen Wiig, Mike Myers, Eddie Murphy, and Will Ferrell. And it has contributed an entire lexicon of instantly recognizable words and phrases for talking about American life. Well, isn't *that* special? In its journey, *SNL* has gone from a fledgling cast of Not Ready for Prime Time Players to a must-see television show with an audience of millions each week. Not to mention a stack of Emmy Awards to its credit, a Peabody Award, and three Writers Guild of America Awards. It's been ranked as one of the greatest shows of all time and has been inducted into the National Association of Broadcasters (NAB) Broadcasting Hall of Fame. *SNL* is *the* gold standard of American TV sketch comedy.

CATCHPHRASE QUIZ

Test your knowledge of *SNL* catchphrases with this catchphrase quiz! Which *SNL* cast member (or guest host) said the following catchphrases?

a. "It's always something!"

b. "You look mahvelous!"

c. "Yeah, that's the ticket!"

d. "I got a fever, and the only prescription is more cowbell!"

e. "Not gonna do it!"

f. "Touch my monkey!"

g. "Simmer down now!"

h. "New York's hottest club is . . ."

i. "We are from France!"

j. "I'm Gumby, dammit!"

k. "Sometimes when I get nervous, I stick my hands under my arms, and then I smell my fingers . . ."

l. "You can't-a-have-a de Mango!"

m. "Attention, teachers and students!"

n. "Living in a van, down by the river!"

o. "And you are . . . ?"

p. "I'm good enough, I'm smart enough, and doggone it, people like me!"

q. "Baseball's been berry, berry good to me!"

r. "We are . . . two wild and crazy guys!"

s. "Oooh! It's a lady!"

Answer key: a) Gilda Radner, b) Billy Crystal, c) Jon Lovitz, d) Christopher Walken, e) Dana Carvey, f) Mike Myers, g) Cheri Oteri, h) Bill Hader, i) Dan Aykroyd, j) Eddie Murphy, k) Molly Shannon, l) Chris Kattan, m) Chris Farley, n) Chris Farley, o) David Spade, p) Al Franken, q) Garrett Morris, r) Steve Martin or Dan Aykroyd, s) Tim Meadows

FROM SECOND CITY TO *SNL*

The Second City improvisational comedy troupe (which has theaters in Chicago, Toronto, Detroit, and many other cities) has been a source of talent for *Saturday Night Live* from the show's launch in 1975. Folks who've made the leap from "Second Citizen" to "Not Ready for Prime Time Player" include the following people. Their years with *SNL* appear after each name.

- Dan Aykroyd (1975–1979)
- Vanessa Bayer (2010–present)
- Jim Belushi (1983–1985)
- John Belushi (1975–1979)
- Paul Brittain (2010–2012)
- Aidy Bryant (2012–present)
- Brian Doyle-Murray (1980–1982)
- Rachel Dratch (1999–2006)
- Robin Duke (1981–1984)
- Chris Farley (1990–1995)
- Tina Fey (1997–2006)
- Mary Gross (1981–1985)
- Tim Kazurinsky (1981–1984)
- Dave Koechner (1995–1996)
- Tim Meadows (1991–2000)
- Seth Meyers (2001–2013)
- Jerry Minor (2000–2001)
- Bill Murray (1977–1980)
- Mike Myers (1989–1995)
- Mike O'Brien (2013–present)
- Amy Poehler (2001–2008)
- Gilda Radner (1975–1980)
- Tim Robinson (2012–2013)
- Tony Rosato (1981–1982)
- Horatio Sanz (1998–2006)
- Cecily Strong (2012–present)
- Jason Sudeikis (2005–2013)
- Nancy Walls (1995–1996)

SATURDAY WRITE LIVE

Not only did many performers get their start at *Saturday Night Live*, so did many of the most popular and influential comedy writers working today. Some of them stayed behind the keyboard, and others ventured in front of the camera, becoming performers as well as writers. These stellar scribes include the following:

- Andy Breckman, cocreator of the TV series *Monk* (2002–2009)

- Max Brooks, author of the best-selling novel *World War Z* (2007)

- Greg Daniels, creator of the US version of the TV sitcom *The Office* (2005–2013) and cocreator of the TV show *King of the Hill* (1997–2010)

- Larry David, creator-star of *Curb Your Enthusiasm* (2000–present), and cocreator of *Seinfeld* (1989–1998)

- Al Franken, a US senator from Minnesota, formerly a best-selling author, performer, and screenwriter

- Conan O'Brien, host of the late-night TV series *Conan* (2010–present)

- Bob Odenkirk, costar of the TV show *Breaking Bad* (2008–2013)

- Sarah Silverman, star of the Comedy Central series *The Sarah Silverman Program* (2007–2010)

- Robert Smigel, coscreenwriter of *You Don't Mess with the Zohan* (2008) and *Hotel Transylvania* (2012)

- J. B. Smoove, character actor on TV shows such as *Curb Your Enthusiasm* (2000–present), *Everybody Hates Chris* (2005–2009), and *American Dad* (2005–present)

- Emily Spivey, creator of the sitcom *Up All Night* (2011–2012)

SOURCE NOTES

9   Tom Shales and James Andrew Miller, *Live from New York: An Uncensored History of Saturday Night Live* (New York: Back Bay Books, 2002), 332.

14   Ibid., 429.

22   Alessandra Stanley, "Who Says Women Aren't Funny?," *Vanity Fair*, April 2008, accessed September 9, 2013, http://www.vanityfair.com/culture/features/2008/04/funnygirls200804.

22   Jesse David Fox, "The History of Tina Fey and Amy Poehler's Best Friendship," *Vulture.com*, January 11, 2013, http://www.vulture.com/2013/01/history-of-tina-and-amys-best-friendship.html.

22   "A Nonpartisan Message from Sarah Palin and Hillary Clinton," sketch, *Saturday Night Live*, season 34, episode 1532, first broadcast September 13, 2008, by NBC, http://www.nbc.com/saturday-night-live/recaps/?par=Saturday%20Night%20Live%20%7CVideo%7CSite%20Nav%7CEpisode%20Guide%7Cnull%7C1#cat=34&mea=1532&ima=50431.

22   Ibid.

22   Tina Fey, *Bossypants* (New York: Little, Brown, 2011), 144.

23   Donna Kaufman, "Ladies' 'Night'! The 20 Funniest Female Characters on 'SNL,'" *iVillage*, August 22, 2011, http://www.ivillage.com/amy-poehler-amber-one-legged-hypoglycemic/1-b-294000.

25–26   Benjamin Svetkey, "Garrett Morris: An Ex-'SNL' Star Breaks Out on '2 Broke Girls.'" *Entertainment Weekly*, April 6, 2012, http://www.ew.com/ew/article/0,,20582568,00.html.

26   Shales and Miller. *Live from New York*, 405.

26   Ibid., 404.

28   David Hutchings, "Terry Sweeney Opens Some Eyes, and Maybe a Few Minds, as Saturday Night Live's First Lady," *People*, June 2, 1986, http://www.people.com/people/archive/article/0,,20093779,00.html.

29   Jodie Foster at the Golden Globes sketch, *Saturday Night Live*, season 38, episode 1631, first broadcast January 19, 2013, by NBC, http://www.nbc.com/saturday-night-live/recaps/?par=Saturday%20Night%20Live%20%7CVideo%7CSite%20Nav%7CEpisode%20Guide%7Cnull%7C1#cat=38&mea=1631&ima=115532.

29   Ibid.

31   Courtney Garcia, "*SNL*'s Jay Pharoah on a Mission to Bring a Black Woman on Cast: 'They Need to Pay Attention,'" *theGrio.com*, September 27, 2013, http://thegrio.com/2013/09/27/snls-jay-pharoah-on-a-mission-to-bring-a-black-woman-on-cast-they-need-to-pay-attention/.

31   "Michelle Obama at the White House Cold Open," sketch, *Saturday Night Live*, season 39, episode 1646, first broadcast November 2, 2013, by NBC, http://www.nbc.com/saturday-night-live/video/michelle-obama-at-the-white-house-cold-open/n42641/.

34   J. J. Duncan, "10 Awesome Moments in Political Satire, #7: Chevy Chase Redefines Gerald Ford," *Zimbio.com*, July 31, 2009, http://www.zimbio.com/10+Awesome+Moments+in+Political+Satire/articles/9YKaxlCQOJb/7+Chevy+Chase+Redefines+Gerald+Ford.

34   Ibid.

34–35   Chevy Chase, "Mr. Ford Gets the Last Laugh," *New York Times*, January 6, 2007, http://www.nytimes.com/2007/01/06/opinion/06chase.html?_r=0.

35   Ibid.

35   David R. Sands, "As Tina Fey Soars, Sarah Palin Struggles," *Washington Times*, October 8, 2008, http://www.washingtontimes.com/news/2008/oct/8/tina-fey-soars-sarah-palin-struggles/?page=all.

36   Alec Baldwin,. "Palin on *SNL*: What Did You Expect?" *Huffington Post*, October 20, 2008, http://www.huffingtonpost.com/alec-baldwin/palin-on-isnli-what-did-y_b_136186.html.

36 Sands, "As Tina Fey Soars."

39 Nathan Rabin, "Interview: Will Ferrell," *A.V. Club*, February 26, 2008, http://www.avclub.com/articles/will-ferrell, 14204/.

41 Chevy Chase, quoted in Michael Cader, ed., *Saturday Night Live: The First Twenty Years* (New York: Houghton Mifflin, 1994), 13.

41 Shales and Miller, *Live from New York*, 464.

44 Eric Ditzian, "'Parks and Recreation' Star Chris Pratt Talks Amy Poehler, Adorableness and Cracking Some Beers," *MTV Movies Blog, MTV.com*, September 17, 2009, http://moviesblog.mtv.com/2009/09/17/parks-and-recreation-star-chris-pratt-talks-amy-poehler-adorableness-and-cracking-some-beers/.

46 Fey, *Bossypants*, 144.

47 Cader, *Saturday Night Live*, 23.

SELECTED BIBLIOGRAPHY

Cader, Michael, ed. *Saturday Night Live: The First Twenty Years.* New York: Houghton Mifflin, 1994.

Chase, Chevy. "Mr. Ford Gets the Last Laugh." *New York Times*, January 6, 2007. http://www.nytimes.com/2007/01/06/opinion/06chase.html?_r=0.

Fey, Tina. *Bossypants.* New York: Little, Brown, 2011.

Fox, Jesse David. "The History of Tina Fey and Amy Poehler's Best Friendship." *Vulture.com*, January 11, 2013. http://www.vulture.com/2013/01/history-of-tina-and-amys-best-friendship.html

Garcia, Courtney. "*SNL*'s Jay Pharoah on a Mission to Bring a Black Woman on Cast: 'They Need to Pay Attention.'" *TheGrio.com*, September 27, 2013. http://thegrio.com/2013/09/27/snls-jay-pharoah-on-a-mission-to-bring-a-black-woman-on-cast-they-need-to-pay-attention/.

Hinckley, David. "Sentiments of the Moment. The World According to Sinéad O'Connor, 1992." *New York Daily News,* March 14, 2005. http://www.nydailynews.com/archives/news/sentiments-moment-world-sinead-o-connor-1992-article-1.649809.

Itzkoff, Dave. "The God of '*SNL*' Will See You Now." *New York Times,* August 22, 2013. http://www.nytimes.com/2013/08/25/arts/television/the-god-of-snl-will-see-you-now.html?_r=0&adxnnl=1&pagewanted=all&adxnnlx=1378505658-d51fiI7+8bXMGWmK7rhkKA.

Karp, Josh. *A Futile and Stupid Gesture: How Doug Kenney and National Lampoon Changed Comedy Forever.* Chicago: Chicago Review Press, 2006.

Patinkin, Sheldon. *The Second City: Backstage at the World's Greatest Comedy Theater.* Naperville, IL: Sourcebooks, 2000.

Perrin, Dennis. *Mr. Mike: The Life and Work of Michael O'Donoghue—The Man Who Made Comedy Dangerous.* New York: Avon Books, 1998.

Rabin, Nathan. "Interview: Will Ferrell." *A.V. Club*, February 26, 2008. http://www.avclub.com/articles/will-ferrell,14204/.

Radner, Gilda. *It's Always Something.* New York: Simon & Schuster, 1989.

Rock, Chris. *Rock This!* New York: Hyperion, 1997.

Sands, David R. "As Tina Fey Soars, Sarah Palin Struggles." *Washington Times,* October 8, 2008, http://www.washingtontimes.com/news/2008/oct/8/tina-fey-soars-sarah-palin-struggles/?page=all.

Shales, Tom, and James Andrew Miller. *Live from New York: An Uncensored History of Saturday Night Live.* New York: Back Bay Books, 2002.

Smiley, Brett. "*SNL*'s Vanessa Bayer on Miley Cyrus, 'J-Pop America Fun Time Now,' and Google Alerts." *Vulture.com*, January 13, 2012. http://www.vulture.com/2012/01/snls-vanessa-bayer -on-miley-cyrus-j-pop-america-fun-time-now-and-google-alerts.html.

Stanley, Alessandra. "Who Says Women Aren't Funny?" *Vanity Fair,* April 2008. http://www .vanityfair.com/culture/features/2008/04/funnygirls200804.

Svetkey, Benjamin. "Garrett Morris: An Ex-'*SNL*' Star Breaks Out on '2 Broke Girls.'" *Entertainment Weekly*, April 6, 2012. http://www.ew.com/ew/article/0,,20582568,00.html.

Thomas, Dave. with Robert Crane and Susan Carney. *SCTV: Behind the Scenes.* Toronto: McClelland & Stewart, 1996.

FURTHER INFORMATION

Crystal, Billy. *Still Foolin' 'Em: Where I've Been, Where I'm Going, and Where the Hell Are My Keys?* New York: Henry Holt, 2013.

Dratch, Rachel. *Girl Walks into a Bar. . . : Comedy Calamities, Dating Disasters, and a Midlife Miracle.* New York: Gotham Books, 2012.

Farley, Tom, Jr., and Tanner Colby. *The Chris Farley Show: A Biography in Three Acts.* New York: Penguin Books, 2009.

Franken, Al. *I'm Good Enough, I'm Smart Enough, and Doggone It, People Like Me! Daily Affirmations by Stuart Smalley.* New York: Dell, 1992.

Halpern, Charna, Del Close, and Kim Johnson. *Truth in Comedy: The Manual of Improvisation.* Colorado Springs, CO: Meriwether Publishing, 1994.

Libera, Anne. *The Second City Almanac of Improvisation.* Evanston, IL: Northwestern University Press, 2004.

Martin, Steve. *Born Standing Up: A Comic's Life.* New York: Scribner, 2007.

Saturday Night Live
    www.nbc.com/saturday-night-live/
    The official *SNL* website is a great place to learn more about the show, watch episodes, look up your favorite sketches, meet the stars, and more.

Walsh, Matt, Ian Roberts, and Matt Besser. *Upright Citizens Brigade Comedy Improvisation Manual.* New York: Comedy Council of Nicea, 2013.

INDEX

Belushi, John, 4–5, 10–11, 27, 32, 53, 57. *See also* samurai character
Bush, George H. W., impression of, 13, 37
Bush, George W., impression of, 37, 39, 46

Carvey, Dana, 6, 13–14, 29, 37, 48, 49, 56
Chase, Chevy, 33–35, 40–41, 53–54
Clinton, Bill, impression of, 14
Clinton, Hillary Rodham, impression of, 20, 22
comedy: clubs, 47; and improv, 6, 9, 10, 22, 44, 51, 57; and sitcoms, 7, 26–27, 28, 30, 43, 44–45, 54, 55; and sketch, 5–7, 9–19, 21–31, 33–38, 44–45, 49–55; before *SNL*, 6–7; *SNL* impact on comedy culture, 5–7, 9–19, 21–31, 50, 54–55; *SNL* impact on politics, 33–41, 54–55; and stand-up, 9, 10, 26, 27
Coneheads, 8, 10–11, 25, 50
Crystal, Billy, 50, 51–52, 56
Curtin, Jane, 4, 8, 10–11, 25, 40, 54
Cyrus, Miley, 18

diversity, 21–31

Fallon, Jimmy, 26, 30, 41
Farley, Chris, 14–15, 26, 27, 56, 57
Ferrell, Will, 5, 15, 37, 39, 46–47
Fey, Tina: on *SNL*, 5, 21–23, 33, 35–36, 41, 45–46, 57; as an *SNL* writer, 21, 45–46
Ford, Gerald, impression of, 33–36

Hader, Bill, 5, 19, 30, 56. *See also* Stefon
Hammond, Darrell, 14–15

impressions: of actors and musicians, 13–14, 24, 28–29, 51; of celebrities, 9, 13–14, 18, 28–29, 31; of political figures, 13–14, 24, 32, 33–39, 46

Meadows, Tim, 26–27, 46, 48, 57
Michaels, Lorne, 6, 9, 12, 35, 45, 48, 54–55
Morgan, Tracy, 27, 45
Murphy, Eddie: in movies, 50–51; on *SNL*, 5, 12, 25, 29, 50–51, 56
Murray, Bill, 4, 40, 52–53, 54, 57. *See also* slob comedies
Myers, Mike, 6, 15, 29, 48–49, 56, 57

NBC, 5, 6, 16, 19, 42, 44–45, 54
Nealon, Kevin, 14, 48

Obama, Barack, impression of, 24, 37
Obama, Michelle, impression of, 31

Palin, Sarah: impression of, 20, 22–23, 33, 35–36; on *SNL*, 35–36
Pedrad, Nasim, 23, 42
Pharoah, Jay, 24, 29, 31, 37, 56
Poehler, Amy, 5, 20, 22–24, 35–36, 41, 44–46, 49, 57

Radner, Gilda, 4–5, 10–12, 25, 38, 48, 54, 56, 57
Reagan, Nancy, impression of, 28
Rock, Chris, 5, 26–27, 48, 55
Rudolph, Maya, 16, 22–23, 25, 31, 48, 49

Samberg, Andy, 29, 55
samurai character, 10–11
Sandler, Adam, 5, 14–15, 26, 47–48
Saturday Night Live (SNL): and awards, 46, 55; commercials on, 7, 21, 25, 48; and ethnic diversity, 21, 24–27, 31; and gay cast members and writers, 28–31; and gay characters, 29–31; and impressions, 9, 13–14, 23–24, 28–29, 33–39, 46, 51; and improvised sketches, 51; in the 1970s, 6, 10–12, 25, 52–54; in the 1980s, 9, 12–14, 25; in the 1990s, 14–15, 26–27; in the 2000s, 16–19; in the 2010s, 31, 43–55; launch of, 5–12; movies based on, 50; and musical guests, 16, 18; and parody, 12, 14, 16, 21, 25, 28–29, 37, 40–41, 49–50; and politics, 7, 13–14, 20–22, 24, 28, 31, 32–41; and short films, 18–19, 29–30, 50; and women, 21–25, 31. *See also* "Weekend Update"
Shannon, Molly, 15–16, 56
slob comedies, 52
SNL Digital Shorts, 18–19
Spade, David, 14–15, 26, 48, 56
Stefon, 5, 30–31

Thompson, Kenan, 19, 25

"Wayne's World" skits and movies, 29, 49, 50
"Weekend Update," 11–12, 22–23, 25, 30–31, 36, 40–41, 45, 52, 54
Wiig, Kristen, 17–19, 23, 29, 43–44, 55

Zamata, Sasheer, 31

PHOTO ACKNOWLEDGMENTS

The images in this book are used with the permission of: © Igor Stevanovic/Dreamstime.com, p. 1; © Yohsuke Ikebuchi/Flickr/Getty Images, pp. 2–3, 5 (right), 9 (right), 21 (right), 33 (right), 43 (right); © NBC/NBCU Photo Bank via Getty Images, pp. 4–5, 10, 11, 32–33, 38, 40, 62–63, 64; © Alan Singer/NBCU Photo Bank/Getty Images, p. 6, 8–9, 26, 49, 51; © CBS Photo Archive/Getty Images, p. 7; © R. M. Lewis Jr./ NBC/NBCU Photo Bank via Getty Images, p. 13; © Mary Ellen Matthews/ NBC/NBCU Photo Bank/Getty Images, p. 15, 27, 39, 45; © Dana Edelson/ NBC/NBCU Photo Bank via Getty Images, pp. 17, 20–21, 23, 24, 28, 30, 36, 37, 42–43; © Courtesy of YouTube, p. 18; © Budd Williams/NY Daily News Archive via Getty Images, p. 47; © Jacques M. Chenet/CORBIS, p. 50; © Ron Galella, Ltd./WireImage/Getty Images, p. 53.

Front cover: © Chhobi/Dreamstime.com.
Jacket flap: © Igor Stevanovic/Dreamstime.com.
Back cover: © S.Borisov/Shutterstock.com.

ABOUT THE AUTHOR

Arie Kaplan has written jokes and comedy sketches for the television series *TruTV Presents: World's Dumbest. . . .* He has also written humor articles for *MAD Magazine.* Aside from his work as a comedy writer, Kaplan has written numerous nonfiction books for young readers on subjects ranging from the life of Vlad the Impaler to the history of pop music. As a comics writer, he has written comic book stories and graphic novels for DC Comics, Archie Comics, Bongo Comics, IDW Publishing, Penguin Young Readers Group, and other publishers. He is the author of the acclaimed nonfiction book *From Krakow to Krypton: Jews and Comic Books*, which was a 2008 finalist for the National Jewish Book Award. He lives with his family in New York City.